LO

FEB 2 6 2009

WITHDRAWN

D1443885

The ABC Book of American Homes

  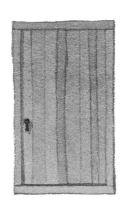  

Michael Shoulders

Illustrated by Sarah S. Brannen

San Diego Public Library
LOGAN   FEB 2 6 2009

✦ Charlesbridge

3 1336 08062 7749

For Jim Vick—M. S.

For my father—S. S. B.

Text copyright © 2008 by Michael Shoulders
Illustrations copyright © 2008 by Sarah S. Brannen
All rights reserved, including the right of reproduction in whole or in part in any form.
Charlesbridge and colophon are registered trademarks of Charlesbridge Publishing, Inc.

Published by Charlesbridge
85 Main Street
Watertown, MA 02472
(617) 926-0329
www.charlesbridge.com

Library of Congress Cataloging-in-Publication Data
Shoulders, Michael.
    The ABC book of American homes / Michael Shoulders; illustrated by
Sarah S. Brannen.
        p. cm.
    ISBN 978-1-57091-565-9 (reinforced for library use)
    ISBN 978-1-57091-566-6 (softcover)
1. Architecture, Domestic—United States—Juvenile literature. 2. Alphabet books.
I. Brannen, Sarah S. II. Title.
NA7205.S54 2008
728.0973—dc22   2007017188

Printed in Singapore
(hc) 10 9 8 7 6 5 4 3 2 1
(sc) 10 9 8 7 6 5 4 3 2 1

Illustrations done in watercolor on Arches paper
Display type set in Nicklas Cochin and Billy and text type set in Cochin
Color separations by Chroma Graphics, Singapore
Printed and bound by Imago
Production supervision by Brian G. Walker
Designed by Susan Mallory Sherman

Americans call many places home. We live in deserts, underground, on water, and in trees. We make homes from plants, mud, metal, and even snow. Let's take a look at some of these homes, from A to Z.

A is for Apartment. All homes in an apartment building share the same roof. Families who live in apartments might have neighbors living beside them, below them, and above them. Some apartments have balconies where families can enjoy the outdoors, even from the tenth floor. What a view!

B is for Beach House. Many Americans make their home on the beach, where they can see and hear the ocean. But living at the beach isn't all smooth sailing. Storms can create huge waves that threaten a house. Many beach houses are built on stilts to allow the ocean to pass safely underneath.

C is for Cajun Cottage. This home is found in southern Louisiana. It is often made from cypress wood, which contains a natural oil that repels insects and keeps the wood from rotting in the damp climate. Because heat rises, the second floor of the cottage is often used for storage instead of living. A porch called a galley runs across the front of this house. During the summer, families can gather on the galley with a cold drink to escape the heat.

D is for Dome House, also called a geodesic home. Although it looks round, it is actually made of hundreds of sturdy, connected triangles. Because of its stability, this house claims the honor of being the strongest house on earth. It has been known to withstand winds of up to 200 miles an hour. Since the walls are curved, the rooms are oddly shaped. Placing furniture can be difficult. Beds and couches may sit out in the open instead of against a wall.

E is for Earth-Sheltered Home. In order to get the most natural light during the day, the south wall is usually made mostly of glass. The rooms in the back of the house may have windows in the ceiling called skylights. Earth-sheltered homes are often constructed of concrete because they have to support several tons of dirt. If you lived in this home, you might need to mow the roof!

F is for Farmhouse. Early colonists built the first American farmhouses over three hundred years ago. These houses were small one-room buildings. Farmhouses today are much bigger. Farm work—milking cows, gathering eggs, planting crops, cutting hay, and feeding animals—begins before dawn and lasts until dark. All this work requires three hearty meals a day, so the kitchen is often the largest and busiest room.

G is for Garage Apartment. The living quarters in this home are built above the garage to save space. These homes are usually near a larger house on the same property. They can be used as a rented home for college students, a first home for small families, or a nearby home for Grandma and Grandpa.

H is for Houseboat. Entire communities live in floating houses in bays, harbors, or wherever there is water. To keep from sinking, large houseboats rest on flotation devices. Sometimes they are even built on floating concrete platforms. There are no yards to mow or leaves to rake when you live in a houseboat. You can catch your dinner from the porch and have waves rock you to sleep at night.

I is for Igloo. I is also for Inuit. The Inuit people live in the Arctic in modern houses. During long hunting trips, Inuits build temporary igloos out of blocks of icy snow. Living in an igloo is not as cold as it might seem. Body heat and lamps warm the igloo from the inside. Too much heat, though, and the igloo melts. For this reason, a small hole in the ceiling allows hot air to escape.

J is for Junk House. This type of house is made of materials that most people send to the dump. The shingles on the roof might be recycled rubber. The family may walk on carpet made from discarded soda bottles. Cotton rags and pieces of old denim jeans may be used between the walls for insulation. The hardwood floors might be made from pine trees killed by beetles. A junk house proves that one person's trash is another person's treasure.

K is for Kilbourne. Sears, Roebuck and Company sold this build-it-yourself home between 1921 and 1929. The Kilbourne was one of the 370 models that Sears offered. Sears claimed the average homeowner could build one of their homes in about three months. The Kilbourne arrived in a kit of 30,000 pieces, often delivered by railroad boxcars. Nationwide, nearly 67,000 Sears homes still stand today.

L is for Log Cabin. Over 300 years ago, when trees were plentiful, Swedish immigrants built the first log cabins in America. Settlers cut trees down and stacked them to make walls. But round logs roll! So the builders notched the ends of the logs with special cuts called saddle notches. Since logs do not lie evenly against each other, the spaces between the logs had to be filled with mud, clay, and moss. This prevented wind from blowing into the house.

M is for Mobile Home. Mobile homes first appeared in the United States in 1933 and were made to be towed easily from one place to another. If families decided to move for a new job or for a change of scenery, they could take their home with them. As time went on, mobile homes got bigger and more difficult to move. Now some people call these houses manufactured homes. Mobile homes are more affordable than traditional houses and are found all over America. If you see one on the highway, watch out—wide load!

N is for Neoeclectic Home. *Neo* means *new* and *eclectic* describes something that is taken from different sources. Neoeclectic architects use bits and pieces of several architectural styles to create a new look. Neoeclectic homes are often called hodgepodge houses.

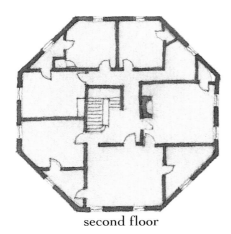

second floor

O is for Octagon
House. This house has eight sides.
If you looked down on an octagon house
from an airplane, you would see that it is
shaped like a stop sign. An octagon house is
much bigger on the inside than a rectangular
house built with the same amount of wall
material. Most octagon houses have a center
room with a circular staircase. Odd-shaped
rooms spread out from the center
room like spokes on a wheel.

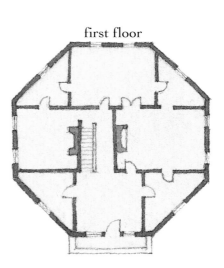

first floor

P is for Pueblo. These communal homes were invented by the Pueblo Indians of America's Southwest. Pueblos are apartment-like dwellings with thick walls of adobe, a mixture of dirt, clay, and straw. Since pueblos are made of earthen materials, rain can damage them. For that reason, pueblos are built in very dry places. Although some pueblos are painted, many owners leave them their natural color. These pueblos blend into their surroundings as if they sprang from the earth.

Q is for Quonset Hut. These circular homes are modeled after a traditional type of Native American lodge. Instead of animal skins covering wooden poles, however, Quonset huts are built with sheets of metal over a steel frame. The U.S. Navy built the first Quonset huts in Quonset Point, Rhode Island, as a cheap and fast way to house large numbers of sailors. Quonset huts are still used today for homes, sheds, garages, workshops, and even airplane hangars!

R is for Recreational Vehicle, sometimes called an RV. Some RVs are motorized, while others are towed behind a car or truck like a mobile home. A mobile home is often a main residence that stays in one place for a long period of time, but RVs are on the go! Some families need to move a lot, and some like to go camping or drive long distances on vacation. An RV allows these families to take their home with them. RVs use limited space efficiently. With bunk beds and unique storage spaces, an RV can provide living space for a family of eight.

S is for Straw House. The first little pig had a great idea—he just didn't build it right. Today's straw houses are constructed of hundreds of bales of straw held in place, like shish kebabs, by metal or bamboo stakes. The bales are covered inside and out with plaster. The result is a super-insulated and nearly soundproof home. Straw houses benefit the environment because they use less wood and are energy efficient.

T is for Tree House.

Some people really
live their lives "out on a
limb." Tree houses are bolted
directly to trees. If the trees are
not strong enough to hold the home,
pillars provide additional support. Entire
families live in some tree houses. They have
electricity, running water, and all the comforts
of many modern homes.

U is for Unique Home. Not every family lives in a house with four straight walls and a roof. Homes, like people, come in all sizes and shapes. They are limited only by the builder's imagination. Have you ever thought of living in a pyramid? Are kings and queens the only people who live in castles? Is there really a lady who lives in a shoe?

V is for Victorian House. These homes first appeared in America in the mid-1800s. Builders added highly decorative woodwork called gingerbread to the porch trim, doors, and gables. They also added extra turrets, towers, and stained-glass windows.

W is for the White House. This home is over 200 years old. The first residents, John and Abigail Adams, moved in during November 1800. Every president except George Washington has lived here. Only 16 of the 132 rooms are used for living quarters. The White House comes with lots of extras, including a jogging track, a tennis court, a swimming pool, and a bowling alley. It even has its own movie theater!

X is for *Xinfang*, a Chinese word for "brand new home." New homes are like a new start in a person's life. They bring the possibility of new friends, new dreams, and new adventures. Many Americans have come from other countries and bring their customs and traditions with them. Whether it is the Spanish *casa nueva*, the French *nouvelle maison*, or the Chinese *xinfang*, in any language there is no place like home.

Y is for Yurt. This circular dwelling is based on the design of a Mongolian *ger*. In Mongolia nomads travel long distances, taking their houses with them. A *ger* can be taken down or put up in an hour or two. In America a yurt is often used as a vacation cabin. Yurts usually have wooden floors, wood or gas stoves, lanterns, sleeping bags, foam pads, and bunks. Large pieces of fabric on the walls and roof help keep the cold out.

Zzzzzzzzz is for falling asleep in the safety of your own home with family all around. It doesn't matter if your house is large or small, old or new, in a tree or on wheels, on land or water, or even made of junk. Home is where the heart is, and what makes it special are the people you share it with.